MARTIN LUTHER'S THEOLOGY OF ANTITRUST

by

JOHN S. EHRETT

STUDIES IN
PROTESTANT IRENICS
VOLUME 2

Series Editors
S. MARK HAMILTON & RHYS LAVERTY

DAVENANT PRESS
LANDRUM, SC

OTHER TITLES IN THE SPI SERIES

HERMAN SELDERHUIS
Peace from Heidelberg

SIMON BURTON
Participation and Covenant in Puritan Theology

DAVID HAINES
Richard Hooker on Natural Theology and Scripture

ISBN-13: 978-1-949716-70-2
ISBN-10: 1-949716-70-8

Cover design and typesetting by
Rachel Rosales, Orange Peal Design
Proofread by Brooke Williams

PRAISE FOR THIS VOLUME

"John Ehrett here accomplishes two things simultaneously: he both provides a careful study of a historic Protestant figure's teaching on political economy and makes those insights useful to contemporary conversations. Ehrett's work is a model of both kinds of scholarship and deserves attention as an important contribution to ongoing projects of recovery within the Protestant tradition."

—PHILIP BUNN
Assistant Professor of Political Science, Covenant College.

"Most of us think of antitrust law as the domain of attorneys and economists. In Martin Luther's Theology of Antitrust, John Ehrett provides a surprising vantage point from which to consider monopolies, cartels, predatory pricing and the like: theology. Ehrett, channeling Luther, reminds us of a truth long neglected: economic thought will run amiss if it abandons a theological framework. As such, antitrust law is not a morality-free zone. The implications of this approach to economics are far-reaching, radical, and much needed."

—MARK T. MITCHELL
Dean of Academic Affairs, Patrick Henry College

"In this concise book, Ehrett brings together the fields of political theory, theology, and history to present Martin Luther's distinctive insights in a contemporary context. This work is a model of faithful (and distinctively Protestant) Christian intellectual engagement with civic life."

—JORDAN B. COOPER

Fellow of Systematic Theology, Weidner Institute,
Chair of Lutheran Dogmatics,
American Lutheran Theological Seminary

ABOUT THIS SERIES

Studies in Protestant Irenics (SPI) is an ongoing project from the Davenant Press. It comprises short, focused, and insightful scholarly works on a wide range of topics, written by scholars grounded in the rich tradition of Protestant irenicism. This is a tradition which draws confidently from the theological, philosophical, and literary traditions of the whole church, whilst remaining committed to the historic Reformation confessions.

SERIES EDITORS

S. MARK HAMILTON is Editor-in-Chief at the Davenant Press. He is both a contributor to and editor of numerous titles, including *Advent Homilies: John Newton* (forthcoming) with Rhys Laverty. His periodical work has appeared in the *International Journal of Systematic Theology*, *Irish Theologi-*

cal Quarterly, *Neue Zeitschrift für Systematische Theologie und Religionsphilosophie*, *Perichoresis*, *Open Theology*, and most recently, in London Lyceum's *The Ledger*.

RHYS LAVERTY is Editorial and Research Director at the Prosperity Institute. Previously he worked for the Davenant Institute where he edited such titles as *Life on the Silent Planet: Essays on Christian Living from C.S. Lewis's Ransom Trilogy*. He co-edited *Reforming Classical Education* and *Advent Homilies: St. Augustine* with Mark Hamilton. He is a published poet and has written widely on cultural issues for publications including *The Spectator*, *The Critic*, *First Things*, and *Mere Orthodoxy*.

For my children,
whose knowledge of "trust busting"
is as simple as "fighting the bad guys"

TABLE OF CONTENTS

Acknowledgements i

Introduction 1

1 Rise of the Medieval Monopolists 11

2 Luther's Theology of Antitrust 19

3 Theological Foundations of Antitrust Enforcement 33

4 Antitrust Enforcement, Luther's Way 47

5 Luther's Antitrust in the Modern World 59

Bibliography

ACKNOWLEDGEMENTS

This book was the exact opposite of the volume I once set out to write. The day after graduating from law school, I sat down in the Sterling Memorial Library with every intention of discovering how my Lutheran tradition reinforced the principles of contemporary laissez-faire economic theory—principles to which I had a prior loyalty. Imagine my surprise upon learning that Luther's theology did *not*, in fact, support my presuppositions. In fact, it positively rejected them.

That revelation was the first step in an intellectual odyssey that continues to the present, an ongoing project of working out how principles of Christian theology can inform the day-to-day doings of a complex modern political economy. I am most significantly indebted to Justin Bullock, Philip Bunn, and Stephen Gibbs for endless rounds of discussion and debate that have clarified my thinking on this theme. Jack Kilcrease oversaw the original academic research project that eventually became this book.

In the policy realm, I am grateful to Alida Kass, Brad Littlejohn, Daniel Kishi, George Priest, Josh Hawley, Matt Stoller, and Mark Meador for many thoughtful conversations that ultimately resulted in this volume. Thanks also go to Garrett Snedeker and the participants in the James Wilson Institute's alumni conference, where some of the ideas in this volume were field-tested, and to Joshua Schendel and the editors of *Modern Reformation* magazine, where I originally raised the question of Luther's "theology of antitrust." Finally, special thanks are due to my wife Mackenzi, who read and commented on the earliest drafts of this project, and to Mark Hamilton, Rhys Laverty, and the other staff of the Davenant Press for their editing work.

All views in this volume are my own and not those of any institution with which I may be associated.

MARTIN LUTHER'S THEOLOGY OF ANTITRUST

INTRODUCTION

Most Christians—and, to be fair, most specialists in the field—have probably never thought about antitrust as a specifically *theological* topic.

In the simplest terms, antitrust refers to the body of law and policy by which a political authority acts to promote competition in a market economy by breaking up consolidations of private—that is, non-governmental—power. In a free-market economy, where the government doesn't supply (most) goods or services to individual citizens, there's no guarantee that over time, *multiple* suppliers of a good or service will survive the competitive process. Rather, the strongest competitors tend to rise to the top. And when a single supplier of a particular good or service comes to dominate a market, a monopoly has emerged.

Monopolies are powerful, and from the perspective of individual citizens, they are often dangerous. When a single supplier dominates a particular market, the monopolist in question gains the power to unilaterally control purchasers' access to the good or service, including by raising the price of that good or service to whatever level it sees fit. In other words, once a monopolist has driven his competitors out of business, he can raise his prices sky-high and consumers will have no recourse but to purchase from him.

It can be very difficult to disrupt a monopoly once it becomes entrenched. For one thing, a monopolist benefits from economies of scale. By investing in assets such as larger warehouses, or more powerful production technology, it can reduce the per-item cost of producing goods and services to such a point that any competitor would be hard-pressed to match its efficiencies. Similarly, a monopolist has enormous power to secure favorable terms from the suppliers of the inputs, or resources, that it uses to produce its own goods and services. It can even use its market power to effectively block suppliers from providing inputs to potential competitors, by simply saying it will refuse to do business with any supplier that "breaks faith" in this way.

Antitrust law is a response to the problem posed by monopoly—or, in more theoretical terms, it is a response to the possibility that free-market competition may paradoxically create a situation where *no* competition actually exists. Over the course of American history, antitrust law was famously deployed against John D. Rockefeller's Standard Oil company, the great railway conglomerates of the Gilded Age, and (later) the Bell System of telephone companies. More recently, many on both the political left and right have argued that powerful technology companies, such as Meta and Google, represent monopolists of the digital age.[1]

Antitrust does not intuitively *feel* like a topic about which the Christian tradition has much to say, beyond the basic moral duties of fair dealing and honesty. And there is good reason for this. While not unknown to the ancients, monopoly is a problem that seems distinctly "modern," a challenge of contemporary markets that lies downstream of the end of Christendom and the "medieval synthe-

1. See, e.g., Tim Wu, *The Curse of Bigness: Antitrust in the New Gilded Age* (New York: Columbia Global Reports, 2018) (making a version of this case).

sis" of politics and theology. And indeed, the world has changed since then. A new language—the language of economics—has largely displaced theology as the basic "grammar" by which human social affairs are described. Even if the very concept of "corporations"—subsistent legal bodies extended in time—is an inheritance of the Christian intellectual tradition,[2] the question of corporate power is debated today in a milieu altogether devoid of theological reference points. The basic normative questions of antitrust are posed squarely within what Charles Taylor has described as the "immanent frame": a context of human affairs conducted on the basis of standards wholly internal to itself, with no reference to transcendent considerations.[3]

Contemporary currents in antitrust law and policy illustrate this. For decades, the main ideological cleavage in the discipline has lain between professed conservatives concerned that antitrust

---

2. See John Ehrett, "*The Myth of Citizens United*," *Anchoring Truths* (July 8, 2024), https://www.anchoringtruths.org/the-myth-of-citizens-united/ ("For Blackstone, when the law on the books treats political and religious authorities as 'corporations,' it merely *recognizes* something, some quality of inherent extension in time, that already exists. It doesn't create anything new.")

3. See Charles Taylor, *A Secular Age* (Cambridge, MA: Belknap Press, 2007), 542.

overenforcement will thwart (immanent) economic growth, and progressives concerned about consolidated private power's ability to thwart (immanent) democratic power. These debates, while inevitably touching on the assertion and counter-assertion of countervailing values, usually come couched in a language of social-scientific objectivity, rapidly progressing into consideration of highly technical questions of market definition, market share, and price effects (among other factors).

It was for this reason that, in 2005, Herbert Hovenkamp—by acclamation, the most prominent antitrust scholar living today—could boldly pronounce that "[a]ntitrust is an economic, not a moral, enterprise," without any "moral content of its own."[4] Hovenkamp's view is not isolated. It is widely shared by mainstream theorists and practitioners in the field.

That is a bold claim. And it is a historically idiosyncratic one, because a closer look at the intellectual history reveals that antitrust law did not emerge from a vacuum. Rather, antitrust represents the latest development of a long history of *moral*

4. Herbert Hovenkamp, *The Antitrust Enterprise: Principle and Execution* (Cambridge, MA: Harvard University Press, 2005), 10, 47.

critiques of monopolistic conduct, particularly within the Protestant tradition.

Largely lost to history is the fact that Martin Luther himself was the foremost Protestant critic of early modern monopolies—the very same kind of monopolies whose existence and effects gave rise to the antitrust laws that remain vigorously debated today. Though Luther obviously does not use the jargon of the modern field, the *referents* of his theological-economic analysis—that is, the forms of business conduct in question—are the very same practices that modern antitrust law exists to punish. In particular, Luther wrote sharply against those who would control commodity supplies and engage in predatory pricing, driving smaller merchants to ruin and consolidating control over particular markets.

But there's an important twist. Luther's arguments for *why* antitrust enforcement is important have little to do with the standard concepts that the field relies upon today—detailed analyses of market concentration, price effects within particular markets, and so forth. Instead, Luther's claims have an explicitly theological cast to them. That is to say, Luther appeals *directly* to principles drawn from Scripture and the Christian tradition in making his arguments *against* monopolistic conduct and in *favor* of vigorous "antitrust enforcement" by the appropriate authorities.

Existing Luther scholarship largely references his views on trade and monopoly merely in passing—as one aspect of his social teachings, or as an interesting footnote in the history of contemporary capitalism's emergence. Indeed, it is *de rigueur* among many writers to situate Luther, like all Protestants, at the head of a historical process through which modern *laissez-faire* capitalism comes into being alongside the waning of ecclesial authority and the breakdown of Christendom. Lost to view, in such treatments, are the ways in which Luther anticipates *specific* types of anticompetitive conduct and the variety of theological rationales Luther deploys to critique them. Even more obscure are the implications of Luther's thinking on this particular issue for contemporary political-economic debates—and, perhaps more importantly, for the life of the church.

This book exists to change that. In what follows, I will argue that Luther's "theology of antitrust," as articulated across his works, represents a serious effort to bring explicit theological categories to bear on the processes of "immanent" economic life, within the contexts of both church and state. Where so many theologians and scholars have defined Luther by his dualisms, this volume argues that in his "theology of antitrust," Luther articulates a vision far more *holistic*.

In the first two chapters, I place Luther's critique of monopoly into historical context, before turning to a detailed theological analysis of his writings on monopoly.[5] This analysis takes up, in turn, (1) the discrete forms of economic conduct that Luther sought to denounce, (2) the theological principles underlying Luther's attacks on anticompetitive conduct, and (3) the temporal and spiritual mechanisms by which Luther envisioned the principles of antitrust being enforced. In the two chapters that follow, I will examine Luther's views on antitrust in view of the dominant assumptions of the modern field, before considering some practical effects of any retrieval effort for policymakers and Christian communities alike. Ultimately, this book contends that Luther advances a distinctively *Christian* vision of antitrust, one that favors active

---

5. A preliminary treatment of these issues can be found in John Ehrett, "Martin Luther's Theology of Antitrust," *Modern Reformation* (June 3, 2022), https://modernreformation.org/resource-library/web-exclusive-articles/martin-luthers-theology-of-antitrust/.

enforcement by civil authorities alongside a policy of rigorous church discipline of would-be monopolists. By current standards, that is a radical proposal indeed.

CHAPTER 1

RISE OF THE MEDIEVAL MONOPOLISTS

Christian histories of the Reformation, and the ideological developments that came with the eclipse of "Christendom," often—understandably—focus more on theological concepts than material processes. For centuries, this history has shaped the constitutive narratives of the various Protestant confessional traditions. But an emphasis on ideas can sometimes (unintentionally) obscure the fact of other major social changes, and Christian reflection upon them—reflection that, perhaps paradoxically, may be *more* relevant to contemporary questions of "Protestant retrieval" than the political-theological developments of early modernity. It's my contention in this book that Luther's thinking on antitrust and monopoly represents just such a reflection, one ripe for critical retrieval today.

Luther's views on monopolistic conduct developed against a backdrop of major economic upheaval. The general problem of monopoly, to be sure, was not a novel one. Concerns over anticompetitive economic conduct dated back at least as far as the days of Greece and Rome,[1] and the Christian tradition had previously taken a hard line towards monopolistic and profiteering behavior.[2] But in Luther's day, the issue had become positively urgent.

A confluence of factors contributed to the nascent monopoly crisis. Geopolitically, new opportunities for foreign trade were becoming available to European merchants, and in order to capitalize on these opportunities, trading companies became increasingly consolidated—pooling their resources in order to offset the increased costs associated with

---

1. David von Mayenburg, "*Wörter für Wucher: Ius commune* and the Sixteenth Century Debate on the Legitimacy of South German Trading Houses," in *Migrating Words, Migrating Merchants, Migrating Law: Trading Routes and the Development of Commercial Law*, eds. Stefania Gialdroni, Albrecht Cordes, Serge Dauchy, Dave de Ruysscher, and Heikki Pihlajämaki (Leiden: Brill, 2019), 181–85.

2. Von Mayenburg, "*Wörter für Wucher*," 191.

ever-more-distant trading.[3] Once that consolidation had begun, it was hard to stop: what began as cost-sharing efforts promptly evolved into outright monopolistic behavior on the parts of the largest companies.[4] Against these powerful firms, small merchants had little chance for survival.[5]

The problem of monopoly extended beyond the international front, however. Increasingly, individual citizens were engaging in anticompetitive behavior independently of the large trading firms, seemingly perceiving no conflict between their Christian theological commitments and their conduct in the market. One contemporary source describes a resident of Augsburg, "Hochstätter," who "had the reputation of being a good Christian, yet he often oppressed the common man. He would buy up at good bargains all the ash-wood, corn, and wine, and keep them in storage till a great demand

---

3. Jacob Salwyn Schapiro, "Social Reform and the Reformation," in *Studies in History, Economics and Public Law, Vol. 34*, eds. Faculty of Political Science of Columbia University (London: P.S. King & Son, 1909), 298–99. See also Roy Pascal, "Martin Luther and His Times," *Science & Society* 2 no. 3 (1938): 335 (discussing commodity monopolies in Reformation-era Germany).

4. Schapiro, "Social Reform and the Reformation," 299.

5. Schapiro, "Social Reform and the Reformation," 299.

arose for them when he would sell at very high prices."[6] This is quintessentially monopolistic behavior.

Imperial authorities were not oblivious to their subjects' concerns, particularly where the large trading firms were concerned. In 1512, the Diet of Cologne took action to officially outlaw monopolies—albeit in exceedingly vague terms that forbade the "dishonorable dealings" and "injurious traffic" of the "great trading companies."[7] The Diet's proscription on monopolies was never enforced, however, leading to the topic's recurrence at the Diet of Nuremberg in 1522.[8] The Nuremberg Diet subsequently created an investigative committee and solicited reports on the monopoly issue from a number of major German cities, including Ulm, Frankfurt, and Augsburg.[9] While Ulm's response urged a moderate antitrust policy that would restrict the number of stakeholders in trading companies, Augsburg's answer was an outright defense of the existing monopolies: "It is impossible to limit the size of the companies, for that would limit busi-

6. Schapiro, "Social Reform and the Reformation," 300.

7. Schapiro, "Social Reform and the Reformation," 307.

8. Schapiro, "Social Reform and the Reformation," 307.

9. Schapiro, "Social Reform and the Reformation," 307–08.

ness and hurt the common welfare; the bigger and more numerous they are the better for everybody."[10] In other words: the bare fact of monopoly isn't really a problem at all.

Undeterred by Augsburg's appeal, the Diet of Nuremberg went on to pass an early antitrust law, which included a requirement that "no commodity shall be entirely under one control" and imposed explicit size thresholds on trading companies: "No merchant shall buy during a single quarter of a year more than 100 [hundredweight] of pepper, 100 [hundredweight] of ginger and 50 [hundredweight] of other spices."[11] But just like the Cologne Diet's directive, this law went largely unenforced, in part due to corrupt arrangements in which city authorities received kickbacks from dominant firms.[12]

Meanwhile, ordinary Germans struggled. Germany in the early sixteenth century was experiencing colossal inflation—in some cases exceeding one hundred percent—which was, rightly or wrongly, perceived as a consequence of overconcentration

10. Schapiro, "Social Reform and the Reformation," 309.

11. Schapiro, "Social Reform and the Reformation," 311.

12. Schapiro, "Social Reform and the Reformation," 312.

in the market.[13] This economic crisis engendered widespread public frustration,[14] which likely led Luther to take up the subject of monopoly explicitly in his own writing.

Luther's interest in the topic was not unusual for his time. While monopolistic conduct is a theme rarely touched by modern church scholars, originally it was theologians and economists—rather than lawyers—who most vigorously examined the question.[15] Critiques of monopoly can be found in the writings of medieval theologians like Jean Gerson, Henry of Langenstein, Henry of Oyta, and Nicole Oresme,[16] and the canon law of the period generally identified monopolistic behavior as a subcategory of financial sin in general (*turpe lucrum*).[17] Accordingly, it is unsurprising that Luther would frame his critiques of monopo-

---

13. Schapiro, "Social Reform and the Reformation," 301–03 ("Other causes operated as well, such as the increase in demand due to the growth of prosperity").

14. Bernd Mertens, *Im Kampf gegen die Monopole. Reichstagsverhandlungen und Monopolprozesse im frühen 16. Jahrhundert* (Tübingen: Mohr, 1996), 10.

15. Von Mayenburg, "*Wörter für Wucher*," 206.

16. Von Mayenburg, "*Wörter für Wucher*," 206.

17. Von Mayenburg, "*Wörter für Wucher*," 193, 203.

listic behavior in explicitly theological (rather than conventionally economic) terms.

Luther's core writings on the subject of anti-competitive conduct span several decades of his career. His best-known works on the topic are the 1519 *Short Sermon on Usury* and 1520 *Long Sermon on Usury*, which were collected together and published as *On Trade and Usury* (*Von Kauffshandlung und Wucher*).[18] Twenty years later, in 1540, Luther published the much lengthier *Admonition to the Clergy to Preach Against Usury* (*An die Pfarrherrn wider den Wucher*).[19] A close look at these texts reveals Luther's distinctive—and provocative—approach to antitrust, from its theological justification to its enforcement strategy.

For Luther, the market isn't something that can be merely left to its own devices—in Hovenkamp's formulation, an "economic" domain from which "moral" considerations can be evacuated. Rather, the importance of Christian wisdom goes all the way down.

18. Hans Wiersma, "Luther on Lending: A Pastoral Response Regarding the Subject of Usury," *Word & World* 30 no. 2 (2010): 193 n.4, 198.

19. Wiersma, "Luther on Lending," 193 n.4.

CHAPTER 2

LUTHER'S THEOLOGY OF ANTITRUST

So after all that: what exactly did Luther have to say about monopolies and their evils?

This chapter answers that question in two steps. First, it considers the specific economic *practices* or *behaviors* that Luther condemned and explains how those practices might be redescribed (or "re-narrated") within the terms of modern antitrust theory. Luther's language at times is imprecise, but the conduct at issue is plainly recognizable as anticompetitive behavior by contemporary standards. Second, this chapter will consider the principal *theological rationales* that Luther deployed in support of his critiques—rationales that diverge sharply from the values typically employed in modern antitrust analyses.[1]

LUTHER ON MONOPOLISTIC BEHAVIOR

Across his various writings on political economy, Luther identifies three distinct forms of economic behavior that can be classified under the rubric of "monopolistic conduct": (1) traditional monopoly behavior, or the practice of dominating the market for a particular good by operating as the sole *seller* in that market; (2) cartelization, or anticompetitive collusion between firms in a given market; and (3) predatory pricing, or conduct that tends to create traditional monopolies by driving competitors out of the market. Each warrants consideration in turn.

1. Traditional Monopolies

The classical targets of antitrust enforcement are traditional monopolies—that is, firms that have

---

1. As a methodological matter, while the preceding section addressed the historical context within which Luther worked, for the most part this section will be concerned to expound Luther's theology of antitrust as a unified whole. The question of how Luther's social doctrines evolved over the course of his lifetime has already been treated extensively by others, albeit not with a specific eye to his views on antitrust and monopolies.

grown so large that they are the sole sellers of a particular product in a given market and hence can command whatever prices they choose to charge. In *On Trade and Usury*, Luther expressly identifies traditional monopolies as subjects of his economic critique:

> [T]here are some who buy up the entire supply of certain goods or wares in a country or a city in order to have these goods entirely under their own control; they can then fix and raise the price and sell them as dear as they like or can. Now I have said above that the rule by which a man may sell his goods as dear as he will or can if false and un-Christian. It is far more abominable that one should buy up a whole commodity for that purpose. Even the imperial and secular laws forbid this; they call it *monopolia*, i.e., transactions for selfish profiteering, which are not to be tolerated in country or city.[2]

2. Martin Luther, "On Trade and Usury (1524)": vol. 45, p. 262, in *Luther's Works, American Edition,* vols. 1–30, ed. Jaroslav Pelikan (St. Louis: Concordia, 1955–76); vols. 31–55, ed. Helmut Lehmann (Philadelphia/Minneapolis: Muhlenberg/Fortress, 1957–86); vols. 56–82, ed. Christopher Boyd Brown and Ben-

Here, Luther identifies the cornerstone of traditionally monopolistic behavior—dominance in a given market—and its concomitant harm, price increases that have a detrimental impact on consumers. And this critique of traditional monopoly extends beyond this form of profiteering within domestic markets. Indeed, Luther subsequently expands the analysis to accuse foreign trading companies of engaging in the same sort of market-dominating conduct:

> Who is so stupid that he cannot see that the trading companies are nothing but pure monopolies? Even the temporal laws of the heathen forbid them as openly harmful to the whole world, to say nothing of divine right and Christian law. They control all commodities, deal in them as they please, and practice without concealment all the tricks that have been mentioned. They raise or lower prices at their pleasure. They oppress and ruin all the small businessmen, like the pike, the little fish in the water, just as if they were lords over God's creatures and immune

---

jamin T.G. Mayes (St. Louis: Concordia, 2009–), hereafter *LW.*

> from all the laws of faith and love. So it happens that all over the world spices must be bought at whatever price they choose to set, and they vary it from time to time.[3]

As before, Luther describes a mode of economic behavior—"control[ing] all commodities" and "deal[ing] in them as they please"—that ultimately culminates in merchants "rais[ing] or lower[ing] prices at their pleasure."[4] For Luther, traditional monopolies are illicit irrespective of national origin.

Luther does, however, contemplate an exception to this general critique of market-controlling behavior: mass purchases by the relevant civil authority as a means of hedging against potential disaster. To draw out that point, he closely analyzes the example of Joseph in the book of Genesis through an economic lens. Luther explains that Joseph "gathered up all the grain in the country and afterward, in a time of famine, [and] bought with it for the king of Egypt all the money, cattle, land, and people," behavior that on Luther's own

3. *LW* 45:270–71.

4. *LW* 45:270–71.

analysis "certainly seems to have been a monopoly, or selfish profiteering."[5] However, Luther immediately emphasizes that "Joseph's transaction was no monopoly" because he "prevented no one else from buying during the good years" prior to catastrophe.[6] Here, Luther appears to construe Joseph's act of gathering up the grain as a *nonexclusive* gathering of grain: Joseph was merely "set[ting] aside a store . . . out of the yield of the common market, or the yearly income which everyone has."[7] This is to say, the claim that *the grain which Joseph had gathered up was, in the wake of famine, all the grain in the country* is not equivalent to the claim that *Joseph gathered up all the grain that was on sale at a given point*, and Luther reads the Genesis account as making the former claim. Modern economic analysis would draw a distinction here—properly speaking, Joseph's transaction was no *monopsony*, or sole-buyer arrangement—but the point is immaterial.

More importantly, Luther explains that Joseph's conduct failed to constitute a problematic monopoly for two reasons. First, Joseph's actions

5. *LW* 45:262–64.

6. *LW* 45:263.

7. *LW* 45:263.

were taken for the sake of the public good: "The text does not say that he alone bought up the grain, but that he gathered it into the king's cities. . . Accumulation of this sort is not self-interest or monopoly, but a good and proper Christian foresight for the good of the community and for others."[8] Second, Joseph did not corner the market for the purpose of his private gain. According to Luther, "Scripture does not tell us that Joseph gathered grain in order to sell it as dearly as he pleased; the text clearly says that he did it not from greed but that land and people might not perish."[9] By contrast, a "greedy merchant sells as dearly as he pleases, seeking only his own profit, and regardless of whether land and people thereby perish."[10] To the extent that intent matters, Luther reasons that Joseph's conduct does not amount to traditional monopoly in the proper sense of the term.

Despite this defense of Joseph's actions, Luther's overall assessment of Joseph's conduct is decidedly ambivalent. He writes that Joseph's success at bringing "all the money and cattle—and all the

---

8. *LW* 45:263.

9. *LW* 45:263.

10. *LW* 45:263.

land and people besides—into the king's possession, certainly does not seem to have been a Christian act, since he ought to have given to the needy without return, as the gospel and Christian love instruct us."[11] In other words, Luther is critical of Joseph's willingness to exploit the circumstances of mass famine as a means of exerting *political* control over vast swathes of the Egyptian populace. Even so, Luther writes of Joseph that "he did right and well" in "administering the temporal government in the king's stead" because "the world ought not and cannot be ruled according to the gospel and Christian love, but by strict laws and with sword and force, because the world is evil."[12] One could read Luther's comments here as an implicit moral critique of the nationalization of industry, but accompanied by a pragmatic acknowledgement that such actions may be necessary *in extremis*. That question, however, ranges beyond the scope of antitrust proper.

2. Cartelization

Modern antitrust enforcement does not target only traditional monopolies, but also "combination[s] .

11. *LW* 45:263.

12. *LW* 45:264.

. . in restraint of trade."[13] While the precise philosophical contours of this notion have proven hard to establish,[14] the general principle is straightforward: if the firms that comprise a given market coordinate to keep prices high, consumers may be compelled to pay artificially inflated prices for goods and services. In a competitive market, conversely, firms have an interest in attracting business by offering goods and services at lower prices. This kind of collusion between firms, or cartelization, is a pathology with which Luther was acquainted:

> Here is another piece of selfish profiteering: Three or four merchants have in their control one or two kinds of goods which others do not have, or do not have for sale. When these men see that the goods are valuable and are advancing in price all the time because of war or some disaster, they join forces and let it be known to others that the goods are much in demand, and that not many have them for sale. If they find any who have these

13. 15 U.S.C. § 1 (Sherman Act).

14. See Oliver Black, *Conceptual Foundations of Antitrust* (Cambridge, UK: Cambridge University Press, 2005), 184–93.

> goods for sale, they set up a dummy to buy up all such goods. When they have cornered the supply, they draw up an agreement to this effect: since there are no more of these goods to be had, we will hold them at such and such a price, and whoever sells cheaper shall forfeit so and so much.[15]

Cartelization, like traditional monopoly behavior, raises costs to ordinary buyers—and can sometimes even lead to additional deceptions, such as "straw purchasing" intended to further cement market control. This, for Luther, is altogether unconscionable.

3. Predatory Pricing/ Conduct Tending to Create a Monopoly

Most antitrust enforcement today does not take the form of high-profile "trust-busting" or the court-ordered breakup of established mega-firms.[16] Rather,

15. *LW* 45:266.

16. See, e.g., Rory Van Loo, "In Defense of 'Breakups': Administering a 'Radical' Remedy," *Cornell Law Review* 105 (2020): 1957 (noting that "the dominant view" is that "breakups are 'radical' and too costly" as well as "too difficult for the government to administer").

a great deal of modern antitrust law has a prophylactic function: it bars the type of conduct that *tends to create* monopolies.[17]

One such form of anticompetitive conduct is predatory pricing—operating at a loss in order to drive competitors out of business and then raising prices once a monopoly has been obtained. A notable recent instance of alleged predatory pricing involved the ride-sharing app Uber: for several years, Uber allegedly operated at an enormous financial loss in order to offer low prices that could undercut the entrenched taxi industry in major cities and maximize Uber's market share.[18] Once the ride-sharing market was sufficiently disrupted, Uber then allegedly raised its prices far beyond their prior points in order to hopefully recoup its losses and generate revenue.[19]

---

17. See, e.g., 15 U.S.C. § 13 (Clayton Act).

18. See Parveer S. Ghuman, "Analysis of Competition Cases Against Uber Across the Globe," *CUTS International* (March 2017), https://www.cuts-ccier.org/pdf/Analysis_of_Competition_Cases_Against_Uber_Across_the_Globe.pdf, 3–4.

19. Ghuman, "Analysis of Competition Cases Against Uber Across the Globe," 3–4.

Luther is evidently aware of this type of predatory-pricing practice and its tendency to create monopolies, and he explicitly denounces it:

> Some [bad actors], when they see that they cannot otherwise effect their selfish profiteering transactions and establish their monopolies because others have the same goods and wares, proceed to sell their goods so dirt cheap that the others cannot meet the competition, and are forced either to withhold their goods from sale, or to face ruin by selling them as cheaply as their competitors do. Thus, the greedy ones get their monopoly after all.[20]

A would-be monopolist, thwarted in his initial pursuit of market dominance, may try to force his competitors to operate at a loss, driving them out of business altogether—conduct which Luther condemns in the strongest possible terms. Those engaged in such behavior, according to Luther, "are not worthy to be called human beings or to live among men; they are not even worth admonishing

---

20. *LW* 45:264–65.

or instructing."[21] Particularly egregious, for Luther, is their willingness to operate at a loss for the sake of acquiring monopoly power: "[T]heir envy and greed is so open and shameless that even at the cost of their own losses they cause loss to others, in order that they may have the whole place to themselves."[22]

In sum, the three kinds of anticompetitive behavior that Luther identifies and denounces—traditional monopoly, cartelization, and predatory pricing—are all behaviors that modern antitrust law also proscribes. But Luther's own critique of these practices goes beyond merely simple accusations of "greed" or generalized economic harm. There is a specifically *theological* cast to Luther's understanding of the need for antitrust, one that warrants a closer look.

---

21. *LW* 45:264–65.

22. *LW* 45:265.

CHAPTER 3

THEOLOGICAL FOUNDATIONS OF ANTITRUST ENFORCEMENT

Luther's general interest in policing anticompetitive market conduct has very little to do with market efficiency or with maximizing his nation's gross domestic product. Rather, his principal concerns are expressly moral and theological.

Luther is explicit about this, explaining that his principal goal is "to speak about the abuses and sins of trade, insofar as they concern the conscience. The matter of their detrimental effect on the purse we leave to the princes and lords, that they may do their duty in this regard."[1] Such a mode of critique is relatively unfamiliar today: while some antitrust scholars do treat the rise of mega-firms as a failure of democratic governance,[2] and so implicitly as a sort of moral problem, none *explicitly* rely on the kind of theological apparatus with which Luther is working.[3]

The identification of three distinct theological harms underpins Luther's critique of monopolistic behavior: (1) egocentrism, culminating in the implicit usurpation by monopolists of God's authority over His creation; (2) the profound failure of neighbor-love associated with anticompetitive conduct;

1. *LW* 45:247.

2. See, e.g., Lina Khan, "The New Brandeis Movement: America's Anti-Monopoly Debate," *Journal of European Competition Law & Practice* 9 no. 3 (2018): 131.

3. In his groundbreaking study of the theological roots of Scandinavian social democracy, Robert Nelson has described the normative foundations of Nordic political economy as "implicit Lutheranism"—that is, grounded in a "strong sense of a common social identity that brings the citizens of the social democratic states together to form a single national community," over against "the Calvinist autonomy of the individual and skepticism of state authority." Robert H. Nelson, *Lutheranism and the Nordic Spirit of Social Democracy: A Different Protestant Ethic* (Aarhus: Aarhus University Press, 2017), 271, 277. Nelson's analysis, however, does not carry forward this insight to the specific topic of antitrust.

and (3) monopolists' implicit arrogance in the face of God's providential will.

1. Egocentrism

According to Luther, monopolistic behavior is not merely immoral because it emerges from the sin of greed, but also because it reflects a disordered and egocentric relation between creatures and their Creator. As Luther writes in his critique of traditional monopolists, "such merchants act as if God's creatures and God's goods were created and given for them alone, as if they could take them from others and set on them whatever price they chose."[4] He echoes that same motif in his denunciation of monopolistic behavior by foreign companies, complaining that they "oppress and ruin all the small businessmen, like the pike the little fish in the water, just as if they were lords over God's creatures and immune from all the laws of faith and love."[5]

Luther identifies two distinct vices in these passages, both stemming from the core error of egocentrism: the tendency to see oneself as a principal and privileged subject of God's creation, and the

4. *LW* 45:262.

5. *LW* 45:270.

tendency to see oneself as exercising authority over creatures that is not properly one's own authority. Against these tendencies, Luther stresses that the subjects of trade are "*God's* creatures and *God's* goods."[6] The monopolist who controls all goods and services within a particular market sets himself up as either a privileged subject of, or an authoritarian stand-in for, the universal origin that is God. Such a monopolist is, in turn, inclined to view himself as "immune" from moral duties.[7] He sins in so doing.

The driving economic principle that follows from Luther's argument here appears to be that *whatever ownership relation is conferred by the concept of private property, it cannot be an absolute moral right to dispose of goods as one sees fit.* Rather, this right must always be understood as restricted by two considerations: the origin of creatures in God, which is a universal origin that transcends any individual proprietor, and the moral constraints imposed by "the laws of faith and love."[8] Anticompetitive conduct is egocentric, and so represents a distorted and sinful understanding of that property right.

6. *LW* 45:262 (emphasis added).

7. *LW* 45:270.

8. *LW* 45:270.

2. Failure of Neighbor-Love

Luther treats anticompetitive market behavior as not merely an outgrowth of sinful egocentrism, but also as a failure to properly love one's neighbor.[9] In one sense, this is almost self-evident: predatory pricing and the cost spikes associated with monopolistic behavior obviously inflict harm on buyers and communities, especially the poor. And Luther certainly describes traditional monopolies as "selfish profiteering"[10] and characterizes the behavior of monopolistic trading companies as "such a bottomless pit of avarice and wrongdoing that there is nothing in it that can be discussed with a good conscience."[11]

Luther's understanding of how far monopolists' failure of neighbor-love extends, however, is surprisingly broad. Neighbor-love in the context of antitrust, for Luther, must extend *even from one competitor to another.*

The claim that a Christian businessperson could have a moral duty not to drive his rivals out of business is an audacious one. But it is a position

9. On this point, see also Esa Mangeloja, "Martin Luther's Business Ethics and the Economic Utopia," *Journal of Economics, Theology and Religion* 3 no. 1/2 (2023): 8.

10. *LW* 45:262–63.

11. *LW* 45:270.

Luther stakes out. Luther's attack on traditional monopolies notes that unduly dominant firms necessarily "*oppress and ruin all the small businessmen*, like the pike the little fish in the water."[12] The "little fish," here, are the competitors to those monopolistic companies. Similarly, Luther argues against predatory pricing by pointing out that its victims—that is, the competitors of the firm engaged in such pricing—"cannot meet the competition, and are forced either to withhold their goods from sale, or to face ruin by selling them as cheaply as their competitors do."[13]

Luther's notion that "competitor welfare" must factor into any moral critique of monopoly is consistent with his larger philosophy of economics. In the course of commenting more broadly on trade and usury in his *Long Sermon*, Luther critiques any "refusal to extend this giving"—that is, concern for the other's financial welfare—„to enemies *or opponents*. It comes hard to our false nature to do good to them who have done evil to us."[14] For Luther, though, this mandate follows plainly from the

12. *LW* 45:270 (emphasis added).

13. *LW* 45:264.

14. *LW* 45:282.

words of Scripture. "[T]here is no getting around it, the commandment has reference to all men, 'Give to him who begs from you'; it is clearly expressed in Luke 6, 'Give to everyone who begs from you.' There is no exclusion here of enemies or opponents; indeed, they are included."[15] Likewise, for Luther, economic counterparties on the opposite sides of purchase transactions must be identified as one's neighbors. While "it may be assumed that with his purchase the buyer is seldom if ever seeking and desiring the welfare and advantage of his neighbor—the seller—as much as or more than his own," it is nonetheless the case that "natural law says that what we wish and desire for ourselves, we shall wish and desire for our neighbor also."[16] The mandate of neighbor-love, in short, is comprehensive.

In light of these principles, Luther's theology of antitrust appears to embed the tenet that anti-competitive conduct is immoral because, in destroying the business of one's competitor, it fails to love that competitor as one's neighbor —even where that competitor is, formally speaking, one's economic opponent.

---

15. *LW* 45:282–83.

16. *LW* 45:307.

3. Arrogance In the Face of God's Will

Luther's final—and perhaps most unusual—theological justification for antitrust enforcement is that, in allowing excessive hedging against circumstantial risk, monopolistic conduct reflects a certain arrogance in the face of the divine will. Notably, this kind of arrogance is distinct from egocentrism in the sense of a conscious displacement of divine prerogatives. Rather, this arrogance is a kind of existential self-satisfaction in one's own (economic) works, an undue confidence in the face of uncertainty.

Luther's clearest statement of this theological harm emerges in the course of his attack on the foreign trade companies' monopolistic practices:

> This year they raise the price of ginger, next year that of saffron, or vice versa; so that in the end it all comes out the same: they do not have to suffer any loss, injury, or risk. If the ginger spoils or they have to take a loss on it, they make it up on saffron, and vice versa, so that they make sure of their profit. All this is contrary to the nature, not only of merchandise, but of all temporal goods, which God wills should be subject to risk and uncertain-

> ty. But they have found a way to make safe, certain, and continual profit out of unsafe, uncertain, and perishable goods; though because of it all the world must be sucked dry and all the money sink and swim in their gullets.[17]

From a contemporary standpoint, Luther's argument here *against* such conduct may seem unintelligible. Hedging against downside risk, after all, just seems like sound business dealing. What could possibly be wrong with practices intended to secure a safe, reliable rate of return?

- But Luther is writing as a theologian, not as a business executive, and his motivations are different—as well as consistent with his broader theological orientation. On Luther's account here, there seems to be some theological significance to the persistence of economic risk—such that one might even say that a perfectly efficient, loss-free economy would not be a *God-honoring* economy.

---

17. *LW* 45:270–71.

Luther's "pro-risk" argument here, specifically in the antitrust context, is left somewhat opaque. However, his specific theological motivations surrounding this point come to the fore elsewhere in his economic writings. In critiquing the practice of making oneself a "surety"—that is, staking one's own person as collateral for a loan—Luther denounces those so engaged as "act[ing] as though they didn't even have to consult God on the matter or give thought to whether they are even sure of a tomorrow for their own life and property."[18] Such self-satisfaction is tantamount to "act[ing] without fear of God, as though [the individuals involved] were themselves the source of life and property, and these were in their own power as long as they themselves willed it. This is nothing but a fruit of unbelief."[19]

Why such harsh words? Accusing economically self-assured individuals of full-on "unbelief" is, of course, a weighty charge. Yet such self-assurance, Luther insists, is diametrically opposed to the proper attitude that a Christian ought to adopt: "God is an enemy of that assured, unbelieving presumption

18. *LW* 45:254.

19. *LW* 45:254.

which forgets him; therefore, he opposes it in all that he does, lets us fail and stumble, snatches away life and property when we least expect it[.]"[20]

Luther urges his readers to take a different path. Christ's instruction to believers in the Lord's Prayer is merely to ask for *daily* bread, "so that we may live and act in fear, and know that at no time are we sure of either life or property, but may await and receive everything from his hands, as a true faith does. And truly we see it every day in many of God's works, that things must work out a certain way whether we like it or not."[21] The Christian engaged in economic life must at all times be viscerally conscious of the sheer contingency of his well-being—and on the basis of that apprehension, rely faithfully on God.[22] Indeed, such contingency may play a vital pedagogical role in the believer's formation: Luther observes that if God "did not let us experience injustice and trouble, the human heart could not maintain itself; it becomes too deeply enmeshed in temporal things

20. *LW* 45:255.

21. *LW* 45:255.

22. See also Sean Doherty, *Theology and Economic Ethics: Martin Luther and Arthur Rich in Dialogue* (New York: Oxford University Press, 2014), 31–32 (discussing, as a general principle of Luther's economic ethics, the motif of dependence upon God as provider).

and too firmly attached to them. The result is satiety and disregard of the eternal goods in heaven."[23]

In short, a believer ought to "fear [God] and [be] content with the present and rejoice[] in it," since "all man's undertakings and presumption are sheer vanity, and nothing but toil and evil, unless God is brought into them."[24] Economically speaking, "presuming upon the future," or "trusting in any man or in oneself" reflects a lack of trust in God; the only proper posture is "clinging to God alone."[25] Thus, on Luther's account, the monopolist who stores up for himself vast quantities of goods is the *consummate* self-assured unbeliever.

Taken together, Luther's normative theological arguments for antitrust enforcement—the need to resist egocentrism, the need to promote neighbor-love even toward one's business rivals, and the need to preserve a state of affairs in which one immediately depends upon God—diverge starkly from contemporary justifications for antitrust, which focus almost exclusively on price effects and market efficiencies. Luther, in short, is concerned with

23. *LW* 45:280.

24. *LW* 45:255.

25. *LW* 45:257.

human beings' relationship to *God*—a consideration which naturally works itself out in the realm of human affairs. Sins against God in the economic context are always also sins against one's neighbor.

This is ultimately why, for Luther, monopolistic behavior is a problem in the first place. It isn't just that monopoly power thwarts democratic responsiveness, suppresses innovation, or increases prices—though it may in fact do all of those things. That is a language of abstraction that obscures the real relationships affected by anticompetitive conduct. Luther is concerned with the fact that monopoly power involves exploiting one's consumers *and one's competitors* in a misguided bid to usurp the prerogatives of God Himself.

It follows from this that monopolistic behavior can't just reduce to "good business sense" that operates in a realm evacuated of Christian moral commitments. For Luther, anticompetitive dealing is as much a spiritual problem as it is a mathematical one.

So what should be done about it? The next chapter takes up that question directly.

CHAPTER 4

ANTITRUST ENFORCEMENT, LUTHER'S WAY

Luther's treatment of the evils of monopoly power does more than merely identify the problem. He has plenty of thoughts on how to *combat* it, too. And the scope of Luther's concept of antitrust enforcement was expansive indeed. To wit, Luther was not content merely to relegate antitrust enforcement to the civil authorities; a close reading of his work suggests that Luther viewed monopolistic behavior as something that *ecclesiastical* authorities should also punish. In other words, because antitrust violations are not merely violations of positive law, but sinful in themselves, *Luther's writings on economic policy support the radical conclusion that the moral principles of antitrust should be enforced not just by the state, but also by the church.* Monopolists should not fear only fines, but *excommunication.*

Start with the easy part—the role of temporal power. When the subject of monopolistic behavior comes up, Luther is unambiguous in his view that civil authorities ought to prohibit it directly. For Luther, the proper function of civil authorities is not to spiritually chastise those engaged in anticompetitive behavior, but rather to address their "detrimental effect on the purse"—that is, the economic harms they are inflicting.[1] The kind of authority required to do so, Luther surmises, must be "a strict, harsh temporal government which will compel and constrain the wicked to refrain from theft and robbery[.]"[2]

And Luther's approach is indeed strict and harsh. Where traditional monopoly behavior is concerned, Luther argues that "[p]rinces and lords would punish it and put a stop to it if they really wanted to do their duty."[3] Latent here is the implication that because such conduct presently exists,

1. *LW* 45:247.

2. *LW* 45:258.

3. *LW* 45:262.

the civil authorities are, at the time of writing, *failing* to properly do their duty.

Luther reserves his severest criticisms, though, for those engaged in predatory pricing with the intent of establishing a monopoly. "The temporal authorities would do right," Luther opines, "if they took from such fellows everything they had, and drove them out of the country."[4] The modern term for a legal remedy on this scale is "disgorgement," or the turning-over of all of one's ill-gotten gains. Disgorgement damages are uncommon today, however, due to their severity[5]—and Luther's proposal for punishment of those engaged in predatory pricing goes much further, all the way to the *total* forfeiture of one's assets and banishment from the regime. Severe as it is, though, the internal logic of this approach is straightforward enough.

But *how*, exactly, should authorities go about implementing these norms? Luther's writings outside the explicit context of monopoly again provide helpful clues. Methodologically, Luther argues that

---

4. *LW* 45:265.

5. See, e.g., Caprice L. Roberts, "Restitutionary Disgorgement for Opportunistic Breach of Contract and Mitigation of Damages," *Loyola of Los Angeles Law Review* 42 (2008): 144, 174–75 (discussing the infrequency of disgorgement as an ordered remedy).

laws against economic malfeasance ought to be clear and straightforward, rather than overly complex and nuanced. He is well aware that line-drawing under imperfect conditions is a difficult task: "How can anything which the world must use in this wretched life be purified in the impure law?"[6] However, this does not mean that rules shouldn't exist—indeed, whatever law is promulgated should be readily intelligible. "It is sufficient for it to be a blunt, plain, and simple law. It cannot be subtle and sharp, or else it will become so notched that it cannot even cut butter when it ought to split apart stumps and logs."[7] When this principle is transposed into a contemporary antitrust context, it seems likely that Luther would have favored "brightlines" in the antitrust context—such as market concentration thresholds and categorical prohibitions on particular forms of conduct[8]—over circumstance-bound, multifactorial analyses.

Of course, for Luther no human law can ever be perfect. "Secular law is a weak, petty, polluted

6. "To Pastors, That They Should Preach Against Usury (1540)," in *LW* 61:292.

7. *LW* 61:292.

8. *LW* 61:295.

law that expends great effort to maintain temporal peace and the life of the belly in order to increase and sustain mankind, for the sake of the saints unto yonder eternal life."[9] This should not deter civil authorities, however, from enforcing the law as best they can: civil law "cannot restrain all sins, but only as many as possible."[10] Imperfect enforcement of the law is acceptable, even inevitable, since human beings live in a morally fallen world. Far worse would be a world where no laws at all were enforced.[11]

Luther's understanding of the appropriate scope of antitrust enforcement, however, ranges well beyond the civil law courts. Indeed, it appears to extend to the *pulpit and altar itself*—an extrapolation that is one of the most arresting and unusual features of Luther's theology of antitrust. According to Luther, Christians engaged in monopolistic market behavior ought to face consequences from *both* temporal and spiritual authorities alike.

Luther's views on the spiritual power's enforcement of antitrust principles are most clearly articu-

9. *LW* 61:295.

10. *LW* 61:295.

11. See *LW* 45:258 (enforcement of the law "is necessary in order that the world may not become a desert, peace vanish, and men's trade and society be utterly destroyed").

lated in his 1540 exhortation to pastors to preach against the sin of "usury" from the pulpit. Traditionally, that term refers to the practice of charging interest on loans[12] (or, where weaker anti-usury doctrines are concerned, charging *extortionate* interest).

Evidence suggests, though, that Luther here is using the term "usury" loosely, in such a way that would extend it to monopolistic conduct of the sort condemned in his earlier writings. Early on in his exhortation, Luther condemns those who would "buy up commodities, withhold supplies, create scarcity, raise the price of grain, barley, and everything people are supposed to have, and then wipe their mouth[.]"[13] Further on, Luther pleads with usurers on behalf of the poor, writing that "[i]s it not they who, in the end, cannot hold onto one halfpenny or bit of bread because of your usury since through your usury you drove up and inflated the price of everything?"[14]And shortly thereafter, he

12. See, e.g., Paolo Astorri, "Early Modern Lutheran Theologians and the Redeemable *Census*: Towards a Reformulation of the Interest Prohibition," *Studia Historica: Historica Moderna* 44 no. 1 (2022): 54–56 (considering "usury" in the narrow sense of interest on loans).

13. *LW* 61:288.

14. *LW* 61:324.

returns to the same point: while the prosperous "can manage to endure the inflation caused by your usury, a poor man cannot. He . . . has many children and is unable even to earn bread for them by his grueling labor since your covetousness and usury drive up and inflate the price of everything."[15] From an economic standpoint, the practice of charging interest on loans is not identical with monopolistic commodity purchasing, and interest-bearing loans do not necessarily trigger predatory cost increases in staple goods. This discontinuity strongly suggests that Luther, in his 1540 exhortation to pastors, has in mind monopolistic behavior and is simply using the term "usury" as a catch-all category to refer to economic misconduct writ large.[16]

Pragmatically speaking, what should be done about the problem of usurers—such as monopolists—in the church? Pastors, Luther writes, ought "to admonish parishioners from time to time throughout the year and to instruct them to beware of usury and covetousness so that this scoundrel may be stripped of his mask by which he has

15. *LW* 61:325.

16. Cf. von Mayenburg, "*Wörter für Wucher*," 180 ("A definition of the expression 'usury' is . . . difficult, however, because sources use it with various connotations.").

disguised himself to appear just and good."[17] Here Luther considers and rejects the excuse that sharp economic dealing is simply a harsh reality of the world, with which the church ought to make its peace. "What else is the world but constant indulgence in injustice, covetousness, usury, and every kind of vice and wickedness?"[18] Rather, Christians are called to a higher obligation, which may very well contravene the world's standards. "If you follow the world, you will dwell with it forever in the pit of hell. . . Look not at what the majority or the world is doing but at what is just and what the majority ought to do."[19] In the course of this discussion, Luther also explicitly takes up and rejects the (surprisingly contemporary-sounding) claim that one could "serve one's neighbor" by directing goods and services to their most economically useful ends through unfettered market processes.[20] "You, the preacher, must speak about this and not be silent,

17. *LW* 61:285.

18. *LW* 61:286.

19. *LW* 61:287.

20. See Nelson, *Lutheranism and the Nordic Spirit of Social Democracy*, 118 ("[Luther] would have strongly objected to this main premise of Smith's *Wealth of Nations*—the pursuit of self-interest as an 'invisible hand' that worked for the good of all.").

but point out to the people clearly and distinctly that what is done against God's Word and the law is not described as a service or good deed."[21] Economic ends, in short, do not justify economic means where Christian morality is concerned.

Where admonitions like these prove ineffective, Luther advocates for a ratcheting scale of intimidatingly punitive sanctions. First, pastors "should confidently reprove and condemn usury from the pulpit," making absolutely clear that economic misconduct is indeed sinful.[22] Second, where a pastor has "certain knowledge of any such person" embroiled in misconduct, he "should not give him the Sacrament nor the Absolution as long as he does not repent" or else risk "mak[ing] [one]self a participant in his usury and sin and go[ing] to the devil with him."[23] Third, "when he dies, unless he has repented, [a pastor] should leave him alone as a pagan and not bury him among Christians nor accompany him to the grave."[24] In sum, to the extent such a person fails to "acknowledge his sin and

21. *LW* 61:289.

22. *LW* 61:301.

23. *LW* 61:301–02.

24. *LW* 61:302.

repent," he is rendered "a usurer and idolater in service to Mammon, he is an unbeliever; cannot have neither forgiveness of sins, the grace of Christ, nor the communion of the saints; and is in no position to receive the same, but has condemned, cut off, and excommunicated himself[.]"[25] Where economic sins are concerned, the church's most fearsome penalties are available.

In sum, for Luther, antitrust appears to be a matter of eternal, not merely temporal, significance. Hovenkamp's amoral vision of antitrust could not be further away. When viewed as a whole, Luther's theology of antitrust constitutes an intricate framework of prohibitions, justifications, and enforcement mechanisms that contemporary Protestants have left almost entirely unexamined.

Perhaps antitrust—and monopoly power in general—is simply too obscure a topic to fire the minds of many Protestant writers today, even those otherwise engaged in political theology and its retrieval. But I suspect the reason is simpler than that: Luther's paradigm here is impossible to situate cleanly within the left-right binary that has come to be so constitutive of contemporary political debates. Luther articulates a comprehensive theologi-

---

25. *LW* 61:302.

cal vision of political and social reality, alongside an insistence that the economic realm cannot be "set off" from Christian moral responsibilities—even going so far as to argue that the agonism of market processes must be mitigated by neighbor-love for one's *competitor*. This theological understanding of antitrust stands for a politics all its own.

CHAPTER 5

LUTHER'S ANTITRUST THEOLOGY IN THE MODERN WORLD

Economic theory, like all disciplines, has evolved dramatically over time. From a strictly historicist perspective, it may be easy to classify Luther's approach to antitrust as merely a relic of its time—an interesting historical curiosity but little more.

This final chapter argues otherwise. The account of antitrust that Luther provides is still important today both politically and culturally, particularly in light of recent challenges to established antitrust orthodoxy. This relevance is not merely theoretical: Luther's proposals are specific enough that, even read centuries later, they point towards surprising possibilities for real action on the parts of temporal and spiritual authorities.

REGROUNDING THE PHILOSOPHY OF ANTITRUST

From the perspective of a modern antitrust practitioner, what makes Luther's approach to antitrust so unusual—and, in many ways, inaccessible—is its theoretical foundation. With his overtly theological concerns placed at the fore, Luther is simply not operating according to the paradigm that governs antitrust theory today. He deploys transcendent considerations wholly excluded from modern antitrust law's "immanent frame."

In the United States, the currently dominant value paradigm for antitrust law centers on the concept of "consumer welfare"—a theme most famously stressed by antitrust scholar Robert Bork, who would later be unsuccessfully nominated to the U.S. Supreme Court.[1] Bork held a low opinion of the theoretical trajectory of American antitrust law since its inception, and complained that the lack of consistent standards for adjudication had turned antitrust law into little more than the in-

1. See John Ehrett, "The Bork Paradox and the Conservative Legal Movement," *American Affairs* 5 no. 3 (2021): 54–55.

efficient "harassment of business."[2] In his seminal study *The Antitrust Paradox*, Bork considered and rejected a wide range of potential theoretical justifications for antitrust law before staking out a novel position: consumer welfare—or the effect of market concentration on individual buyers—should be virtually the *only* factor courts should consider in determining whether certain forms of conduct were anticompetitive.[3] In the simplest terms, for Bork high levels of market concentration—that is, the dominance of one or a few firms in a given market—should not be presumed legally problematic *unless* their dominance manifested in the form of increased prices for consumers.[4] Judges' own anti-monopoly instincts should play no part in their

2. Robert H. Bork, *The Antitrust Paradox* (McLean, VA: Bork Publishing, 2021), 2, 6.

3. Bork, *The Antitrust Paradox*, 446 ("[C]ompetition must be understood as the maximization of consumer welfare or, if you prefer, economic efficiency. . . . In a word, the goal is maximum economic efficiency to make us as wealthy as possible. The distribution of that wealth or the accomplishment of non-economic goals are the proper subjects of other laws[.]"). Notably, Bork explicitly rejected the view that "competitor welfare" should factor, in any way, into antitrust adjudication. Bork, *The Antitrust Paradox*, 53 (describing such concerns as, on Bork's paradigm, "mak[ing] impossible antitrust law").

4. Bork, *The Antitrust Paradox*, 446–48.

evaluation of antitrust litigation: in judging antitrust suits, courts should generally rely on highly complex mathematical analyses of defined product markets and defer to experts about the impact of concentration on consumer prices.[5]

Bork's approach soon changed the whole direction of American antitrust law and can readily be correlated with patterns of increased market consolidation across diverse sectors of the American economy.[6] It has not been without its critics, however. In recent years, the ubiquity of the consumer welfare standard has been sharply criticized by a school of reformists known as "New Brandeisians"—named after Supreme Court Justice Louis Brandeis, known for his aggressive trust-busting instincts.[7]

Were he alive today, Luther would probably be unimpressed by the prevailing American approach to antitrust. While a standard of "consumer welfare" could be superficially interpreted as a crude

5. Ehrett, "The Bork Paradox and the Conservative Legal Movement," 57.

6. See Amy Klobuchar, *Antitrust: Taking On Corporate Power from the Gilded Age to the Digital Age* (New York: Knopf Doubleday, 2021), 136–37 (chronicling the decline in antitrust enforcement action that followed the publication of Bork's *The Antitrust Paradox*).

7. See Khan, "The New Brandeis Movement," 131–32.

proxy for the neighbor-love Luther deems so crucial, most of his other driving moral concerns drop out of modern antitrust theory. For one thing, Luther's notion of neighbor-love in the market context extends not only to buyers, but also, as previously noted, to rival sellers—suggesting that a kind of "competitor welfare" analysis is required. Furthermore, by implicitly permitting high levels of concentration in particular markets insofar as prices remain stable, modern antitrust theory does nothing to alleviate the dangers of both egocentrism—belief in lordship that is not properly one's own—and arrogance in the face of existential risk.

Methodologically speaking, these latter concerns on Luther's part are "vertical," or oriented toward the God-man relation, and so altogether absent from "horizontal" understandings of economics that remain confined to the level of the immanent. And it is this broadly premodern orientation that has likely deterred contemporary scholars from seeing Luther's theology of antitrust as in any way relevant to present debates. In one of the only existing works to directly place Luther into conversation with modern antitrust theory, scholars Kenneth Elzinga and Daniel Crane dismiss Luther's analysis of the Joseph story—in particular, the distinction Luther draws between purchases for the public good and those for private gain—as unpersuasive, "[b]ecause antitrust economics does not distinguish whether monopoly profits are used for personal gain or personal philanthropy" and "resource misallocation" results in both cases.[8] But Luther's response to that charge would likely be blunt: Christian economics *should* make such distinctions. Luther's approach is entirely uninterested in baptizing the natural order of things, and far more concerned with ordering those things according to Christian ethics.[9]

Luther would have good reason to stake out such a bold position. After all, if his theological claims are sound, then the principles informing his analysis are not merely contingently true, but *perennially* true. This means that the pragmatic policy conclusions that follow from those principles—

8. Kenneth G. Elzinga and Daniel A. Crane, "Christianity and Antitrust: A Nexus," in *Christianity and Market Regulation: An Introduction*, eds. Daniel A. Crane & Samuel Gregg (Cambridge, UK: Cambridge University Press, 2021), 78.

9. Cf. Klaus K.L. Brockhoff, "A Short Note on Martin Luther's Idea of Business Ethics," *Management & Organizational History* 13 no. 1 (2018): 61 (stressing "Luther's view to embed ethical norms into regulations by authorities that in themselves should be based on Christian ethics").

assuming that in fact they do so follow—cannot logically be refuted by the modern adoption of a "consumer welfare" analysis. The consumer welfare approach is a product of its time and embeds normative judgments of its own, such as the implicit notion that "ease of consumption" is the only relevant antimonopoly consideration.[10] Luther rejects that particular normative judgment and argues for his own: that even in the civil sphere, authorities should regulate market conduct in a manner consistent with Christian theological commitments.

In short, the fact that modern antitrust theory has "moved beyond" appeals to the transcendent in no way rules Luther's own moral approach out of bounds. It simply means that a different metaphysical orientation now informs the law. One could certainly argue that Luther's pragmatic conclusions do not follow from his theological premises, but that is an altogether different question and one not generally on the table in contemporary debates.

---

10. Cf. John Milbank, *Theology and Social Theory: Beyond Secular Reason*, 2nd ed. (Malden, MA: Blackwell Publishing, 2006) ("[B]y asking about what *must* emerge and so be valued," social theorists, including economic theorists, tend to "deduce values from the facts, rather than recognizing certain cultural facts . . . as inherently involving certain evaluative and ideological descriptions").

How would antitrust policy, as administered by temporal and spiritual authorities alike, likely look different today if Luther's paradigm had been carried through to the present?[11] On such a model, civil authorities' antitrust policy would rely on "blunt, plain, and simple law[s]"[12] and impose severe penalties, such as disgorgement damages, on violators.[13] Traditionally monopolistic behavior, cartelization, and predatory pricing would be vigorously policed, though with an eye to the reality that all such enforcement efforts must inevitably prove

---

11. On this point, subsequent research in this area might aim to determine whether patterns of antitrust enforcement in the Scandinavian countries most shaped by political Lutheranism diverge from those in Anglo-American countries. One notable recent survey along these methodological lines, tracking the influence of political Lutheranism on social welfare policy across cultural regions, can be found in Allen Calhoun, "Taxation and Welfare," in *Protestant Social Teaching: An Introduction*, eds. Onsi Aaron Kamel, Jake Meador, and Joseph Minich (Landrum, SC: The Davenant Press, 2022), 215–21. Some limited research does suggest that, at least in Norway and Sweden, national governments took relatively aggressive steps during the interwar period to limit the anti-competitive tendencies of international oil conglomerates. See Päl Thonstad Sandvik and Espen Storli, "The Quest for a Non-Competitive Market: Standard Oil, the International Oil Industry and the Scandinavian States, 1890–1939," *Scandinavian Economic History Review* 68 no. 3 (2020): 298–302.

12. *LW* 61:292.

13. *LW* 45:265.

imperfect. Put simply, antitrust enforcement agencies would likely enjoy more financial support than they do at present and would have clearer statutory mandates.

Assuming Luther's theological concerns with monopolistic behavior are worth taking seriously, political movement in this general direction is both possible and desirable. Contemporary discontent over increasing economic consolidation is beginning to open up new opportunities. Indeed, as if glimpsed dimly through a mirror, traces of Luther's driving theological concerns still show up in modern debates. For example, critics of the consumer welfare standard often appeal to democratic values, on the theory that unitary economic entities *ought not* wield the sort of power that leads not only to market dominance, but also political influence.[14] According to this line of criticism, power should be reserved to the *people* who comprise corporations, rather than the corporations that depend upon human beings for their existence. This argument can

14. Khan, "The New Brandeis Movement," 131 ("Dominant corporations wield outsized influence over political processes and outcomes, be it through lobbying, financing elections, staffing government, funding research, or establishing systemic importance that they can leverage. They use these strategies to win favourable policies, further entrenching their dominance").

be rephrased, and perhaps framed in a more theological way: anticompetitive behavior might be said to entail a kind of illicit egocentrism on the parts of monopolists, an act of *setting oneself up in opposition to the universal origin from which all things emerge.* In modernity, that universal origin is no longer viewed as supernatural—here the *vox populi* stand in for the *vox Dei*—but the general shape of the argument is very close to Luther's. Carl Schmitt's old adage—that all modern political concepts are secularized theological concepts—is well taken.[15]

In a similar vein, pastors who find Luther's theological arguments compelling should have few qualms about preaching boldly from the pulpit against market-related misconduct. Where they are known to the congregation, unrepentant economic predators should face not merely civil sanction, but ecclesiastical discipline. Faithful handling of the Word and Sacraments, for Luther, requires no less.

---

15. Carl Schmitt, *Political Theology: Four Chapters on the Concept of Sovereignty*, trans. George Schwab (Cambridge, MA: The MIT Press, 1986), 36. See also Nelson, *Lutheranism and the Nordic Spirit of Social Democracy*, 25 (arguing that "western civilization might still be described as in essence a 'Christian' civilization—even though its Christianity is now frequently presented in newly modern and thus partially disguised forms").

In the end, Hovenkamp's characterization of antitrust law as a sort of morality-free zone is not merely anachronistic: it is wrong. The law of economics, like all law, inevitably enshrines a certain moral vision, and the only salient question is *which* moral vision will ultimately win out. Few approaches to antitrust more clearly typify this principle than Luther's.

Translating Luther's alternative vision of antitrust into a contemporary milieu is difficult, but not impossible. Egocentrism, failure of neighbor-love, and arrogance in the face of uncertainty are as sinful today as they were in Luther's day. They are persistent temptations besetting a fallen human race, and both civil and ecclesiastical authorities have a divine mandate to fight against them. As that battle rages across the economic landscape of the modern age, reclaiming Luther's distinctive understanding of antitrust may be a strategic move well worth making.

CODA: THEOLOGY, ECONOMICS, AND CRITICAL RETRIEVAL

Within Protestant intellectual circles, the last few decades have witnessed a surge of interest in "retrieval" projects. Countless scholars and students now benefit from greater familiarity with primary source texts and a deeper understanding of the ways in which the working presuppositions of the Reformers and their immediate heirs—from classical theism to their understanding of civil power—diverge drastically from modern formulations.

The possibility of *political* retrieval—that is, of carrying elements of Reformational political theories forward into contemporary contexts—has proven to be one of the most controversial and contested aspects of this conversation. That is partly a result of the nature of the subjects involved.[16] While (for example) the recovery of divine simplicity can *immediately* enable ministers of the Word to speak more properly of God's essence and attributes in the context of divine worship, it is much less obvious what an ordinary layperson is to *do* with the proposition that (for example) civil authorities have a moral responsibility to promote right doctrine. It may well be that there are so many confounding variables ("prudential considerations") involved that the proposition doesn't count for very much by

16. See John Ehrett, "The End of Protestant Retrieval," *Ad Fontes: A Journal of Protestant Letters* (Nov. 27, 2024), https://adfontes-journal.com/web-exclusives/the-end-of-protestant-retrieval/.

itself.[17] These variables are not merely incidental to politics; they *are* the stuff of politics, for all intents and purposes. As a result, arguments about Protestant political retrieval regularly engage massive, complex topics like "Christian nationalism," the feasibility of religious liberty and pluralism, and the merits of the American founding—but in ways that are not readily resolvable even by the standards of the discussants' own conditioning tradition.[18]

The interminability of these debates has an enervating effect: where root-and-branch critiques of liberal-democratic order are on the table, near-term political engagement starts to feel pointless. And this tendency is only exacerbated by the *de facto* sequestration of theological issues in contemporary political contexts. Today, questions relating to life, marriage, religious liberty, and the relationship between theology and politics are regularly grouped

---

17. See John Ehrett, "Political Prudence as Fuzzy Thinking," *Ad Fontes: A Journal of Protestant Letters* (Jan. 22, 2025), https://adfontesjournal.com/commonwealth/political-prudence-as-fuzzy-thinking/.

18. Cf. Alasdair MacIntyre, *After Virtue: A Study in Moral Theory*, 3rd ed. (Notre Dame, IN: University of Notre Dame Press, 2007), 222 (explaining that "a living tradition . . . is a historically extended, socially embodied argument, and an argument precisely in part about the goods which constitute that tradition").

together under the single heading of "values issues." Public-facing church and parachurch entities are referred to as "values groups," and most congressional offices have a designated "values staffer" to handle outreach and oversee legislation in this arena. Apart from that, "values" issues don't much enter into the daily operation of government: for all their metaphysical importance, debates over life and marriage represent a vanishingly small part of the business of modern governance. Against such a backdrop, it isn't surprising that interest in "Protestant political retrieval" has often taken on a distinctly reactionary cast. *This is all such a mess. Don't we need to burn it down?*

As this book has hopefully demonstrated, recovering an appreciation of the Reformers' understanding of political economy offers an alternative to this response. This is not a call for a retreat into vague sentimentality: Luther's "theology of anti-trust" is grounded *directly* in his *specifically Christian* commitments, which are worked out in *both* temporal and spiritual settings. Carrying Reformational theological insights "forward" into contemporary life need not involve turning back the clock. There are far more creative possibilities ready at hand.

Ultimately, the antidote to frustration over the "nakedness" of today's public square, and the public marginalization of theologically weighty subjects, is a deeper understanding that *all* political issues, no matter how abstruse, are "values" issues. Aquinas was right: theology is the queen of the sciences. And this should be grounds for hope. It means that key insights of the Protestant intellectual tradition can be realistically brought to bear, *here and now*, upon urgent questions of public order, questions that every political system—no matter how seemingly "secularized"—must confront. Every government has a budget, after all. Its economic decisions are never really neutral.

Even antitrust, that most technical of fields, is no exception.

BIBLIOGRAPHY

Astorri, Paolo. "Early Modern Lutheran Theologians and the Redeemable *Census*: Towards a Reformulation of the Interest Prohibition." *Studia Historica: Historica Moderna* 44 no. 1 (2022): 53–76

Black, Oliver. *Conceptual Foundations of Antitrust*. Cambridge, UK: Cambridge University Press, 2005.

Bork, Robert H. *The Antitrust Paradox*. McLean, VA: Bork Publishing, 2021.

Brockhoff, Klaus K.L. "A Short Note on Martin Luther's Idea of Business Ethics." *Management & Organizational History* 13 no. 1 (2018): 54–64.

Calhoun, Allen. "Taxation and Welfare." In *Protestant Social Teaching: An Introduction*, edited by Onsi Aaron Kamel, Jake Meador, and Joseph Minich, 213–36. Landrum, SC: The Davenant Press, 2022.

Doherty, Sean. *Theology and Economic Ethics: Martin Luther and Arthur Rich in Dialogue.*

New York: Oxford University Press, 2014.

Ehrett, John. "Martin Luther's Theology of Antitrust." *Modern Reformation* (June 3, 2022),

https://modernreformation.org/resource-library/web-exclusive-articles/martin-luthers-theology-of-antitrust/.

Ehrett, John. "Political Prudence as Fuzzy Thinking." *Ad Fontes: A Journal of Protestant Letters.* Jan. 22, 2025. https://adfontesjournal.com/commonwealth/political-prudence-as-fuzzy-thinking/.

Ehrett, John. "The Bork Paradox and the Conservative Legal Movement." *American Affairs* 5 no. 3 (2021): 54–68.

Ehrett, John. "The End of Protestant Retrieval." *Ad Fontes: A Journal of Protestant Letters.* Nov. 27, 2024. https://adfontesjournal.com/web-exclusives/the-end-of-protestant-retrieval/.

Ehrett, John. "The Myth of *Citizens United*." *Anchoring Truths.* July 8, 2024. https://www.anchoringtruths.org/the-myth-of-citizens-united/.

Elzinga, Kenneth G., and Daniel A. Crane. "Christianity and Antitrust: A Nexus." In *Christianity and Market Regulation: An Introduction*, edited by Daniel A. Crane & Samuel Gregg, 74–100. Cambridge, UK: Cambridge University Press, 2021.

Ghuman, Parveer S. "Analysis of Competition Cases Against Uber Across the Globe." *CUTS International* (March 2017). https://www.cuts-ccier.org/pdf/Analysis_of_Competition_Cases_Against_Uber_Across_the_Globe.pdf.

Hovenkamp, Herbert. *The Antitrust Enterprise: Principle and Execution*. Cambridge, MA: Harvard University Press, 2005.

Khan, Lina. "The New Brandeis Movement: America's Anti-Monopoly Debate." *Journal of European Competition Law &* Practice 9 no. 3 (2018): 131–32.

Klobuchar, Amy. *Antitrust: Taking On Corporate Power from the Gilded Age to the Digital Age*. New York: Knopf Doubleday, 2021.

Luther, Martin. *Luther's Works, Vol. 45: The Christian in Society II*. Edited by Jaroslav Jan Pelikan,

Hilton C. Oswald, and Helmut T. Lehmann. Philadelphia, PA: Fortress Press, 1999.

Luther, Martin. *Luther's Works, Vol. 61: Theological and Polemical Works*, Edited by Benjamin T. G. Mayes and Christopher Boyd Brown, trans. Matthew Carver. Saint Louis, MO: Concordia Publishing House, 202.

MacIntyre, Alasdair. *After Virtue: A Study in Moral Theory*, 3rd ed. Notre Dame, IN: University of Notre Dame Press, 2007.

Mangeloja, Esa. "Martin Luther's Business Ethics and the Economic Utopia." *Journal of Economics, Theology and Religion* 3 no. 1/2 (2023): 1–22.

Mertens, Bernd. *Im Kampf gegen die Monopole. Reichstagsverhandlungen und Monopolprozesse im frühen 16. Jahrhundert.* Tübingen: Mohr, 1996.

Milbank, John. *Theology and Social Theory: Beyond Secular Reason*, 2nd ed. Malden, MA: Blackwell Publishing, 2006.

Nelson, Robert H. *Lutheranism and the Nordic Spirit of Social Democracy: A Different Protestant Ethic*. Aarhus: Aarhus University Press, 2017.

Pascal, Roy. "Martin Luther and His Times." *Science & Society* 2 no. 3 (1938): 332–347.

Roberts, Caprice L. "Restitutionary Disgorgement for Opportunistic Breach of Contract and Mitigation of Damages." *Loyola of Los Angeles Law Review* 42 (2008): 131–76

Sandvik, Päl Thonstad, and Espen Storli. "The Quest for a Non-Competitive Market: Standard Oil, the International Oil Industry and the Scandinavian States, 1890–1939." *Scandinavian Economic History Review* 68 no. 3 (2020): 289–305

Schapiro, Jacob Salwyn. "Social Reform and the Reformation." In *Studies in History, Economics and Public Law, Vol. 34*, 275–434. Edited by the Faculty of Political Science of Columbia University. London: P.S. King & Son, 1909.

Schmitt, Carl. *Political Theology: Four Chapters on the Concept of Sovereignty.* Translated by George Schwab. Cambridge, MA: The MIT Press, 1986.

Taylor, Charles. *A Secular Age.* Cambridge, MA: Belknap Press, 2007.

Van Loo, Rory. "In Defense of 'Breakups': Administering a 'Radical' Remedy." *Cornell Law Review* 105 (2020): 1955–2021.

von Mayenburg, David. "*Wörter für Wucher: Ius commune* and the Sixteenth Century Debate on the Legitimacy of South German Trading Houses." In *Migrating Words, Migrating Merchants, Migrating Law: Trading Routes and the Development of Commercial Law*, 176–231. Edited by Stefania Gialdroni, Albrecht Cordes, Serge Dauchy, Dave de Ruysscher, and Heikki Pihlajämak. Leiden: Brill, 2019.

Wiersma, Hans. "Luther on Lending: A Pastoral Response Regarding the Subject of Usury." *Word & World* 30 no. 2 (2010): 191–99.

Wu, Tim. *The Curse of Bigness: Antitrust in the New Gilded Age.* New York: Columbia Global Reports, 2018.

LIBRARY OF EARLY ENGLISH PROTESTANTISM

The Laws of Ecclesiastical Polity: In Modern English, Vol. 1 (Preface–Book IV)

James Ussher and a Reformed Episcopal Church: Sermons and Treatises on Ecclesiology

An Apology of the Church of England

Jurisdiction Regal, Episcopal, Papal

Radicalism: When Reform Becomes Revolution

Divine Law and Human Nature

The Word of God and the Words of Man

In Defense of Reformed Catholic Worship

A Learned Discourse on Justification

The Shining Human Creature: Christian Ethics Vol. 1

Made Like the Maker: Christians Ethics Vol. 2

Christian Moderation

A Dissertation on the Death of Christ

The Word Made Flesh For Us

AMERICAN THEOLOGY SERIES

Communicating God's Trinitarian Fullness: An Exposition of Jonathan Edwards' End for Which God Created the World

Religion and Republic: Christian American from the Founding to the Civil War

DAVENANT GUIDES

Jesus and Pacifism:
An Exegetical and Historical Investigation

The Two Kingdoms: A Guide for the Perplexed

Natural Law:
A Brief Introduction and Biblical Defense

Natural Theology:
A Biblical and Historical Introduction and Defense

DAVENANT RETRIEVALS

A Protestant Christendom?
The World the Reformation Made

People of the Promise: A Mere Protestant Ecclesiology

Philosophy and the Christian:
The Quest for Wisdom in the Light of Christ

The Lord Is One: Reclaiming Divine Simplicity

CONVIVIUM PROCEEDINGS

For the Healing of the Nations: Essays on Creation,
Redemption, and Neo-Calvinism

For Law and for Liberty:
Essays on the Legacy of Protestant Political Thought

Beyond Calvin:
Essays on the Diversity of the Reformed Tradition

God of Our Fathers:
Classical Theism for the Contemporary Church

Reforming the Catholic Tradition: The Whole Word for the Whole Church

Reforming Classical Education: Toward a New Paradigm

OTHER PUBLICATIONS

Enduring Divine Absence: The Challenge of Modern Atheism

Without Excuse: Scripture, Reason, and Presuppositional Apologetics

Being a Pastor: Pastoral Treatises of John Wycliffe

Serious Comedy: The Philosophical and Theological Significance of Tragic and Comic Writing in the Western Tradition

Protestant Social Teaching: An Introduction

Begotten or Made?

Why Do Protestants Convert?

Richard Hooker on Natural Theology

Life on the Silent Planet

ABOUT THE DAVENANT INSTITUTE

The Davenant Institute supports the renewal of Christian wisdom for the contemporary church. It seeks to sponsor historical scholarship at the intersection of the church and academy, build networks of friendship and collaboration within the Reformed and evangelical world, and equip the saints with time-tested resources for faithful public witness.

We are a nonprofit organization supported by your tax-deductible gifts. Learn more about us, and donate, at www.davenantinstitute.org

Made in the USA
Monee, IL
04 November 2026

67387320R10056